Persis Suddeth

Ima Hogg

FIRST LADY OF TEXAS

Ima Hogg

FIRST LADY OF TEXAS

Reminiscences and Recollections of Family and Friends

By Louise Kosches Iscoe

THE HOGG FOUNDATION FOR MENTAL HEALTH

Ima Hogg

FIRST LADY OF TEXAS

Ima Hogg, age 12. *Courtesy Bayou Bend Collection*

I

Almost a century ago a young district at- torney in Mineola, Texas, wrote to his brother, "Our cup of joy is now complete! We have a daughter of as fine proportions and of as angelic mien as ever gracious nature favor a man with, and her name is Ima!" That day—July 10, 1882—also marked the beginning of a legacy to the people of Texas. For the young father was James Stephen Hogg, a man of integrity and high ideals who became Texas' first native-born and one of its most outstanding governors. Above all, he was a man who instilled in his three sons and daughter his concern for the citizens of Texas. No one better carried out this concern than the daughter of whom he was so proud, the almost legendary Ima Hogg.

Ima grew up in the shadow of the State capitol. As a young child her home was the governor's mansion, a home filled with political figures and famous people in drama and the arts as well as old friends. The mansion also abounded with things to delight a child —stables, a playground, a banister to slide down, a menagerie of exotic animals. As a nine-year-old, Ima and her older brother, Will, were among the guests of honor at her father's inauguration as Governor; later, they and their younger brothers, Tom and Mike, were often included at dinners for visiting dignitaries, discovering early to listen and learn from people knowledgeable in a variety of fields.

The Hogg family, left to right: Ima, Will, Tom, Governor Hogg, Mike, Mrs. Hogg. *Courtesy The University of Texas Archives, E. C. Barker Texas History Center*

Young Ima Hogg. *Courtesy Jane Zivley*

Will and Ima sometimes accompanied their father on political trips, for though he was away from home often, the Governor enjoyed his children and liked their companionship. His concern for people—all the people—was impressed on Ima on these trips, particularly during the frequent visits to "eleemosynary institutions," the prisons and hospitals of late 19th century Texas.

The move from the governor's mansion to another home in Austin at the end of their father's term of office did little to disrupt the lives of Ima and her brothers. What did change their lives was the early death of their mother, Sallie Stinson Hogg. In poor health for a number of years, she died in 1895, but her influence on Jim Hogg and the children was never forgotten. Years later Ima wrote of her mother, "She was, more than anything else, a homemaker in every sense of the word. She encouraged and believed in my father's career but she was a very shy person and shrank from all public appearances herself. She loved to make her home one of charm and hospitality. Our only income was my father's salary, which was not large; so my mother had to be thrifty and wise in her expenditures, and yet she always managed to give an atmosphere of bountiful living."

And in a letter to his sister shortly after his wife's death, Governor Hogg wrote, "My ambition is to raise my children after her model. If I succeed the world will be much better for it."

Jim Hogg played an increasingly important role in Ima's life. In 1896, with Will away at school, the

Governor Hogg and daughter, Ima, with Texas Volunteers. *Courtesy The University of Texas Archives, E. C. Barker Texas History Center*

A turn-of-the-century belle, Miss Ima Hogg. *Courtesy Jane Zivley*

former Governor bought a home in Austin, as much for himself as for his children. Here he could entertain friends and his children could maintain their menagerie—a horse, a bear, a fawn, dogs, two ostriches, and a parrot named Jane that shrieked "Papa, Papa" whenever the Governor appeared. And here, for Jim Hogg, Ima reigned as "the sunshine of my household." By this time she was attending Misses Carrington's Preparatory School and devoting a great deal of time to piano lessons, a study begun as a small child and in which she had shown increasing skill and interest through the years.

A few years later she was enrolled at The University of Texas. "No freshman," she recalled, "could have been more immature, more unprepared, or more frightened than I. But I did have three favorite courses, including German, Old English, and psychology. Psychology was under that great pedagogue and lifelong friend, Dr. Caswell Ellis."

She also had many happy times as one of "the girls," five young women who inaugurated the first sorority on campus and who were to remain friends throughout their lives. These friends also had fond memories of Jim Hogg, for Ima was very close to her father, and her friends were his concern too. Every year he hosted a New Year's reception, personally making the eggnog and supervising the girls in all the preparations. They remembered him as strict but never harsh, always kind and affable, and as a man who could not stand camouflage or falseness—"in fact, honesty was his complex." They recalled

Vivian Brenizer and Ima Hogg. *Courtesy Austin-Travis County Collection, Austin Public Library*

7

that he always talked seriously with young people and showed great understanding, and that he had a wonderful sense of humor though never at the expense of others. The girls were treated courteously at the Hogg home, and they always felt welcome.

Music, however, had become Ima's primary interest, and after two years at the University she left for New York City. There she attended the National Conservatory of Music. The family now was physically divided, with the younger boys in boarding school and Will, who had recently earned a law degree from The University of Texas, practicing in Austin, while Jim Hogg was still travelling a great deal to develop a new business venture. But they remained close despite the distances. In a number of letters—and all the family were prolific letter writers—the Governor asked Ima to write to and encourage her younger brothers. Will was more demanding: "Dear Sis, Please do not neglect your duty of writing them [Tom and Mike] a joint letter once a week. Don't forget to write to me once in a while and your dear daddy every day."

Jim Hogg saw to it that the family always had a home to which they could return. This was of great importance to him:

Home! The center of civilization. Home! The pivot of constitutional government. Home! The ark of safety to happiness, virtue, and Christianity. Home! The haven of rest in old age, where the higher elements of better manhood can be taught rising generations by the splendid example of settled citizenship. Every man should have a home!

After moving his family from rented houses to purchased ones as well as in and out of the governor's mansion, after seeing them off to schools and work, he acquired that special home. The Varner Plantation, outside of West Columbia, Texas, fulfilled all his dreams, It was here that his family could gather and he could entertain his friends. It was also here that the Hogg family fortune began.

While Will Hogg worked diligently in his father's law offices in Austin, James Stephen Hogg was busy pursuing an interest in petroleum. This concern came about almost by accident, for Hogg and his partner had purchased land near West Columbia as speculation for land development. Shortly afterward, however, oil was struck at Spindletop—oil in greater quantity than even the speculators had dreamed—and that new field was not a great distance from the Varner Plantation. The magnitude of the discovery and the challenge of capitalizing on it were strong incentive to get into this fledgling industry. The former Governor had noted when he first bought the home that fires flared from the ground when a match was struck. Later he commented on a fine artesian water well that spewed water twenty feet into the air. In a letter to Ima he said, "The oil prospects are good. It may yet turn out to be a gusher of oil."

Hogg never saw the oil strike on the Varner Plantation. With the foresight that characterized his career, however, he stipulated in his will that his children not sell the home for at least 15 years after

Varner Plantation.

Album page of "the girls." *Courtesy Jane Zivley*

10

his death. Within that specified period, in 1919, a rich new oil-bearing sand was discovered. Two years later, the West Columbia oil field was producing 12 million barrels a year. The father's hunches about the land and his dreams of financial security for his children were both fulfilled.

His hopes that his children become concerned, sensitive, and productive citizens also were realized. In a letter to Ima in 1902 he said, "Amidst the vicissitudes of a checkered career, from orphanage in boyhood, I know I have at times done wrong, but never wantonly, wilfully. Looking back I have little to regret. Looking forward I have unshaken hopes that in you and my three boys I shall enjoy much pride and undefiled pleasure in Old Age." He also encouraged her to serve as an example for her younger brothers. "With your acquaintances and large circle of friends in Texas, won by your own exemplary character and excellent behavior, you have nothing to dread in the future, provided that you do not change radically in your disposition and habits. With you or away from you I have every reason to be grateful to God for such a girl."

James Stephen Hogg was known for his unselfish devotion to the people of Texas. Through his sons and especially his daughter, his desire to improve the education and the opportunities of his fellow citizens also came to fruition, far beyond what even he could have foreseen.

West Columbia oil boom. *Courtesy The University of Texas Archives, E. C. Barker Texas History Center*

II

A newspaper article once noted that there were two traits which Governor Hogg shared with other members of his family: they tended to be uncommonly articulate, and they acted on some inner compulsion in accord with the old biblical holding that of those with many talents, much is expected. They also shared an extraordinary talent for communicating their ideas to others. The example was set by James Stephen Hogg; it was ably continued by his eldest son, Will. Ima Hogg revered her father and she adored her older brother. Their example of acting for the betterment of the people of Texas became her lifelong vocation.

"History records many people who have earned distinction by their capacity to visualize and conceive constructive projects, others who have gained honor by their ability to carry out such projects, still others whose financial generosity in support of such projects has brought them widespread respect. Rare indeed, however," said the speaker presenting the Rotary Club's Distinguished Citizen Award in 1969, "are those persons in whom all three of these essential proclivities are abundantly combined. Such a person is Miss Hogg."

When Ima Hogg returned to Houston to live after studying music in New York and Germany, she began her many years of initiating, carrying out, and supporting projects to improve life around her and of inspiring others to follow her example and leadership. The year was 1909. In the three years since their father's death, Will had moved back to Houston to look after the family interests and was fast becoming an astute businessman as well as attorney. Ima was in her mid-twenties, an attractive young woman with blonde hair piled high, an accomplished pianist, modest and somewhat shy yet with a determination and perseverance that were to have a tremendous impact on those around her.

One who knew each member of the family well in those days is Gertrude Vaughn who, as an 18-year-old girl, began working for Miss Ima and remained with her for 55 years. "Mr. Will was the papa," Mrs. Vaughn recalls. "He was all business, everybody's boss, but he was so sweet and good. He gave so much, but he didn't want anybody to know he'd given. And he was always interested in things—he and Miss Ima were very much alike in that way. But," she continued, "what a temper! . . . Mr. Mike was a fun-loving man. He had many friends and they were always having a good time. Mr. Tom wasn't around very much. He was more of a loner who liked cars and horses . . . Miss Ima? All I can say is wrapped up in one thing—I loved her and she loved me."

Music was one of Ima Hogg's primary interests those first years in Houston, and it remained a key source of pleasure for her and, through her, for multitudes of others throughout her life. For some years she taught piano and music to talented scholar-

Ready for the parade. *Courtesy Austin-Travis County Collection, Austin Public Library*

Mike, Ima, and Tom, 1903. *Courtesy The University of Texas Archives, E. C. Barker Texas History Center*

ship pupils, and she helped provide the support for the music education of a few selected young people who showed particular talent. But she had a greater impact on the music world as one of the founders of the Houston Symphony. An old friend from those years still recalls the efforts involved. "I remember the early days when she trudged up and down Main Street getting ads for the symphony programs. My husband was on the board at one time, and she saw to it that he and others spent many hours calling people to try and get new members. Ima had an enormous facility for getting people to work for her. It wasn't that she wasn't hard on you, but she was equally hard on herself."

Music to Miss Ima was always more than a particular score or a single event. Many years later, when she was receiving one of a long string of honors, she spoke to the assembled Houston leaders:

If our symphony is to qualify as an instrument of brotherhood, it must meet certain requirements and expectations. In a world struggling toward peace and a universal humanitarian regard for mankind, there is no place for an aloof or exclusive institution. I must say it has ever been the aim of the symphony to serve as a unifying and democratic agency in our region and city, that music may reach and touch every facet of our civic life.

Music was only one of Ima Hogg's many interests. As a friend remembers, "She was so vitally interested in everything that concerned the city. She kept her brothers interested—they'd do anything for her."

She worked hard to get women on the school board back in the teens when it was considered a very forward idea. We were all in the early movement together as suffragettes, but Ima wanted more than just the vote; she wanted to get improvements in the schools as well."

Her concern for others was fortified by determination and inner strength. She proved this shortly after she moved to Houston, where she lived in a ground floor apartment. She awoke one morning to see a man standing in her bedroom. Not one to be intimidated, she asked clearly, "What are you doing in my room? You have no business being here!" As the man turned from the dresser where he'd been fumbling in the drawers she demanded, "What do you have in your hand?" Then, seeing what it was, she continued sternly, "Bring that to me. Why are you taking my jewelry?" The intruder, by this time far more shaken than Miss Hogg, hesitatingly explained that he was out of work, out of money, and that he wanted her jewelry to sell so he might have money to buy food for his family. "That's no way to do it," said Ima Hogg. "Why didn't you just come and tell us?" With that, she wrote down a name and address, handed it to him and told him to go there that very day to get a job. Later, when asked how she had the nerve to do what she did, she merely said, "He didn't look like a bad man." For her, as for her brothers, people were to be helped in whatever way seemed best.

During World War I oil production began on the Varner Plantation. The Hogg family, with Will in

Miss Ima Hogg with Governor Philip La Follette of Wisconsin and Texas Governor James V. Allred at centennial celebration of Texas Independence Day, 1936. *Courtesy Houston Chronicle*

charge, organized under the name of Hogg Brothers, which included their sister as well. This company provided their base of operation for handling and expanding the newly acquired fortune. It also became the base of their many contributions to The University of Texas and to the people of the state.

Will Hogg, from the death of his father in 1906 till his own death in 1930, assumed primary responsibility for the family. He also assumed responsibility for a large number of people, unknown to him personally, who he believed deserved further education. For the Hogg family shared another trait—they firmly believed that their wealth, which was based not on their efforts but came from the land itself, never really belonged to them. It was almost as if it had been put in their keeping to assure its wise use for the people of the state from which it came.

Thus, among Will Hogg's many contributions to higher learning was the stipulation, made just after the First World War, for the Ex-Students' Association of The University of Texas to give funds to attend the University to any veteran who so requested and who could meet the entrance requirements. The association's secretary was instructed also to help any student in need, whatever the cause or problem. The one specification was that no one be told the source of the money. A hearty man and an extrovert, Will Hogg was nonetheless modest about helping others. His concern was that they be helped, not that he be known for helping them.

Many of Will's charities were anonymous; some,

in which he encouraged the contributions of others, were widely known. He was noted for taking a blank-paged blue book to all of his wealthy friends, seeking their signatures for pledges of large sums of money to benefit one civic project or another which he deemed worthy. He started this practice in support of the Ex-Students' Association, but Houston also benefited greatly from his efforts. A large city park, a museum of fine arts, the YMCA, the Civic Center, and the Houston Country Club were some of the causes receiving support through his one-man fund-raising campaigns.

During these years he also helped and encouraged his sister in beginning her collection of antiques. Among Ima Hogg's earliest memories were the visits to "my Grandfather Stinson's old homestead in East Texas. His house was filled with antebellum furnishings, long out of fashion. Later we lived in the governor's mansion in Austin and when I was still a small child I knew the thrill of sleeping in the old Sam Houston fourposter bed."

She first became interested in collecting English furniture around 1915. Five years later she bought her first American chair, a chair that was a revelation, for it introduced her to the existence of American antiques that were created earlier and in a finer style than the heirlooms from pioneer Texas. At the time she considered the Queen Anne piece quite expensive, in fact "so costly, I couldn't get my brother excited about buying it until he did get interested in it, and then he got very excited about it.

Pursuing civic interests, 1940. *Courtesy Houston Chronicle*

19

Miss Ima, 1950. *Courtesy Gittings Studio*

I told him, 'We have a rare opportunity—to collect American antiques for a museum in Texas. It has never been done before.'" His enthusiasm matched hers until his death, and for a ten-year period they collected the choicest items of early American furniture that could be found.

As the collection grew, finding a place to keep it became a considerable problem. In 1927 they commissioned architect John Staub to design a house that would provide an appropriate background for their acquisitions as well as a home for themselves and their brother Mike. Though the home was lived in for only a short time by her brothers, Bayou Bend became Miss Ima's home for many years and the setting for her prize examples of American heritage.

Bayou Bend was built not as a museum but a home. Yet Miss Ima, as she was increasingly called with affection and respect, remained concerned about the people of Texas. While still living there she planned how to convey the collection and home to the Houston Museum of Fine Arts, and how best to present the many pieces of furniture and art she had collected. Always a perfectionist, she spent ten years planning the presentation, rearranging furnishings according to period, adding on to the house itself, and bringing an antiquarian to Houston to train the first group of docents. No detail was neglected in assuring that the collection was exact in every way. Miss Hogg personally supervised the project and had the final voice in every item selected for display. Her unerring taste and sense of what was best, along with her great knowledge and keen color sense, became almost legendary among those who worked with her. She loved her home, but as she explained to the docents, "When you love something enough it's easy to give it up in order to see it go on."

But that was many years later. While she lived in Bayou Bend, Miss Ima entertained often and well. When the home was first built, a number of neighbors in the River Oaks area where it is located objected to the large number of parties and meetings that were held there. Persuasiveness, however, was one of her many talents, and she soon persuaded them to accept the frequent entertainment. Most of this was not for personal pleasure, though there was some of that, but to bring people together to make things happen. And through a combination of charm and obvious concern, she persuaded these people she assembled to help carry out some of her dreams and the dreams of her father before her.

One reason she was able to expect, and get, so much from others was her selflessness. Everyone who knew Ima Hogg knew that she wanted nothing for herself, not even the publicity. Her wants were for the people of Texas. One admirer credited her with "an exceptional combination of gracious firmness, insistence on seeking perfection, and impatience with obstacles or excuses, untainted by selfishness, and all mellowed by unfailing wit and feminine charm," making her "the hardest lady of my acquaintance to say 'No' to." Others would agree, particularly the gentleman who, after asking Miss Ima to lunch one day in Austin, soon found himself driving 50 miles down the highway to New Braunfels for a bite because she thought it would be a nice place to go. An ulterior motive, he later learned, was to seek a particular antique, but it never occurred to him to say no.

Her ability to persuade others was never idly used by Ima Hogg. She was persuasive in furthering interests that concerned all the people, in developing programs or achieving goals that would contribute toward the betterment of persons throughout the state. One of these interests focused on the fine arts—music, furniture and home furnishings, and the decorative arts. But she had two other abiding interests. One of these was mental health, the other was education; and both were combined with her love for The University of Texas.

III

*Education, and particularly higher educa-*tion as exemplified by The University of Texas, was of great importance to everyone in the Hogg family. Governor Hogg himself set the example. Jim Hogg believed in education as a means of improving one's life as well as of preparing the public for the duties and responsibilities of citizenship. He had faith in the University as the source of advancing the education of the people, and he backed that faith with action on its behalf. "So far as I know," said the Board of Regents chairman in 1890 when Hogg was campaigning for governor, "you are the first prominent statesman of Texas who, in a campaign speech, has had the boldness to speak an earnest word in behalf of the State University; and if you are elected governor, you will be the first one who has committed himself beforehand to the adequate and proper maintenance of this institution since its organization."

Will Hogg continued the tradition. Instrumental in founding the Ex-Students' Association, he used his role as a Texas Ex to help provide an education for needy students. He gave financially to Memorial Stadium, the Student Union, and the campus YMCA. He gave anonymously to those in trouble, saying "Relieve the distress and investigate afterwards. If he is a student of the University and in distress, that is all I want to know." And he gave of his time, always making himself available for everything from helping individual students to defending the University against those who would lower its standards or hinder its progress.

Mike Hogg, like his older brother a graduate of The University of Texas and its Law School, maintained his interest in his alma mater even as he moved from law into business and political activities. He, too, contributed to the University, upholding the example and interest of his brother Will.

Almost always in accord with the interests and concerns of her family, especially her father and her brother Will, Ima Hogg also was concerned with education in all of its many facets. As a resident of Houston she was interested in the universities and colleges of that city and friendly with many of their faculty members, but The University of Texas was always the main institution in her mind. "Most of my compulsions," she commented in later years, "are rooted and grounded in The University of Texas."

She saw a chance for education in more than one setting. She was convinced, for example, that anyone interested in music "has a duty to inspired and gifted young ones. We sometimes do not open our eyes and ears wide enough to perceive the march of the contemporary idiom."

Always one to follow through on her ideas, Miss Ima ran for and won a term on the Houston School Board. "In a weak moment," she wrote to a friend shortly before the 1943 election, "at the request of the Citizen's Educational Committee, I filed for the

Miss Ima during her tenure on the Houston School
Board. *Courtesy Jane Zivley*

University of Texas President T. S. Painter, Miss Ima,
and Dr. Robert C. Cotner at centennial celebration of
Governor Hogg's birth, 1952.

24

School Board election." An old friend remembers, "She was interested in getting a liberal school board, in getting visiting teachers and nurses for the schools. She wanted her brother Mike to run, but he was quite shy; he wouldn't run because he didn't think he could take the abuse of a campaign. She decided she could take it, so she ran and won, but only for one term." The lady mused a moment. "She was called so many things . . . slandered by those who thought her too liberal . . . so she didn't run again."

Miss Ima herself wrote during that time, "Sometimes I am sorely tempted to resign from the School Board for I really don't think I'm suited for that kind of public service. It is too involved with extraneous influences. But then I visit the schools and feel reassured." Times change, and needs with them. But, some 30 years later: "She started art classes in the colored schools," Gertrude Vaughn still remembers with pride.

Though she never again sought public office, Ima Hogg always maintained her interest in education and her delight in young people. In the 1960s she commented, "To me, one of the greatest deficiencies in our present educational system is lack of emphasis on the humanizing of education for the individual so that he has a better understanding of himself and others."

She loved to be with young people, to talk to them, to learn from them, and they in turn learned much from her. Dr. Robert Sutherland once took a University class of 70 students on a field trip to Houston. Miss Ima invited them to tea, playing the piano for them in the living room of her Bayou Bend home. "My only regret about the class tea," she later wrote to Dr. Sutherland, "was that I didn't have more opportunity to get acquainted with some of those charming looking young people."

Her concern for the young was evidenced on a broad scale when, long before such organizations were popular or even in the public awareness, she played a key role in founding the Houston Child Guidance Center. She encouraged the children's concerts started by Houston Symphony conductor Ernst Hoffman, delighting in the fact that he planned programs of music that youngsters could sing along with and understand. And it was young people who she hoped would benefit from a book of her father's addresses and State papers. "If young people," she said in accepting the book in his honor, "who read his papers today can find any direction or inspiration from my father's example and from his words delivered over 50 years ago as recorded in this book, then his endeavors will have been vouchsafed a reward in keeping with his highest aspirations." When praised for helping the young, she merely said, "I only open doors." Miss Ima firmly believed in giving young people a start, but only if they were also willing to help themselves. Their own motivation was needed to follow her initial efforts.

There was nothing nostalgic about Ima Hogg's interest in the young. Never one to look back, she

Presenting to Robert L. Sutherland her father's book
on mental health, 1956. *Courtesy Associated Press*

26

liked being with young people because of their contemporary approach. In many ways she was more in tune with them than with her own generation. "She was mentally young . . . contemporary . . . she stayed current," said one young man. "She had a gift for cutting things off . . . not looking back," said another. "Her interest was in the future, not in the past." Except, of course, the past in the sense of the heritage and tradition that provided a background for bettering life in the present and future. An older friend, looking back many years, recalled that, "We'd talk about everything that was wrong in the world and how to improve things. She was always concerned about improving situations, about bettering things for the future." Her concern was with unsolved problems that needed attention, not with how things were or might have been. She kept up to the minute with everything—music, clothes, problems of the day. When the Beatles first gained fame, much to the displeasure of many older and not-so-old people, Miss Ima announced that she liked their music, that they had style. And she liked dissonant music, composing some herself in her student days long before it was a popularly accepted musical form.

The area in which her many interests came together, in which her contemporary outlook culminated in direction and action far ahead of its time, was the field of mental health. It was at the dedication of McDonald Observatory in 1938 that Miss Ima decided on mental health as the focus for her brother's funds. When Will Hogg died in 1930,

he left the bulk of his estate to the institution he had loved, fought for, and supported for so many years—The University of Texas. Rather than stipulate the exact use of this gift, he had indicated that another family member could determine its use, provided he or she also contribute to the same purpose. Mike Hogg was executor of the estate, their sister an administrator. It was Ima Hogg's decision that resulted in bettering the lives of so many people throughout the state. She explained it this way:

In accordance with this provision [in her brother's will] and also with my numerous discussions with Will prior to 1930 of the common goals we had in mind, I have chosen the field of mental health as the area of support for both our funds. Also, in keeping with his wishes and mine, I have chosen as trustees the members of the Board of Regents of The University of Texas to administer the funds. They have established the Hogg Foundation for Mental Hygiene as the instrument for accomplishing this goal.

And in a letter written the following year she said, "I think The University of Texas has an opportunity through a broad mental health program for bringing great benefits to the people of Texas."

The subject had long been of interest to Miss Ima. As a child travelling with her father she had been introduced to the institutions, especially the State hospitals, schools, and prisons, populated by those in need of better mental health. Governor Hogg himself had expressed interest in this field, particularly in trying to understand and minimize the underlying problems that made such institutions necessary. His knowledge of the topic was advanced for those times, based on, his daughter discovered many years later, a well-thumbed book in his library published in 1898, *Responsibility in Mental Disease* by Henry Maudsley. While attending the University, Ima had been particularly fascinated by psychology and impressed by her professor, Dr. A. Caswell Ellis, a leader in the field who became her lifelong friend. This early and continuing concern took a positive stance in the birth of the Hogg Foundation, dedicated to improving the quality of life, reaching out across the state from its center at the University with new approaches to mental health, not mental illness. She wanted a broad-based program that would be oriented toward education, a program that would cooperate with the medical school but would not be located there. This concept of stressing mental health, in contrast to mental illness and insanity, was a pioneering effort in the late 1930's when the Hogg Foundation came into being.

There was one other person whose efforts were an integral part of the development of the Hogg Foundation, its first director and first president, Dr. Robert L. Sutherland. Between them, one as the ever-interested and increasingly knowledgeable source that made it possible, the other a renowned sociologist and ever-concerned human being, Ima Hogg and Robert Sutherland carried out the dreams of James Stephen Hogg and his son Will as well as those of Ima herself. Their correspondence over the years, unfailingly beginning "My dear Dr. Sutherland" and "Dear Miss Hogg," records a history of the thoughts, the wishes, and the actions that have brought respect and recognition to the Hogg Foundation.

The Foundation began officially in 1940. Will Hogg in his will had expressed the wish to provide lecturers for small towns and rural areas which at that time had little chance to hear outside ideas. That goal became the first project of the Hogg Foundation. One newspaper called them "a new type of circuit rider," those men and women who travelled from town to town and one small community to another, speaking to large and small groups which gathered to hear about this unknown thing called mental health.

Just as Miss Ima stayed abreast of the times, so did the Hogg Foundation. December 7, 1941, caused an abrupt change of pace. Efforts turned to helping resolve problems of men in the armed forces, their wives and children, and difficulties of people working in industry for the first time. With its periodic directional changes and with its many far-reaching endeavors, Ima Hogg was always in touch.

In a letter to the Board of Regents chairman in 1941 she confessed, "I must say, however, in justice to myself, my active interest in the Foundation was never anticipated after the estate was turned over to the University authorities. It is only through the courtesy of Dr. Rainey [University President Homer P. Rainey] and Dr. Sutherland that I have been drawn into discussion of any plans which have been made."

In meetings of the Hogg Foundation as well as of other groups and clubs in which she was interested, Miss Ima stayed more in the background in those earlier years. She was shy by nature and had been overshadowed by her brothers while they were alive, though her influence on them had been a strong one. As the years passed she became more and more outspoken. As her brother Will before her, she stood for what she thought was right and was fearless in letting her views be known. With the Hogg Foundation she wanted the results to be in human terms, not merely in publications, and she was quick to say so. Though she understood research, she was somewhat impatient of it. As she wrote to a University regent, "The members of our family have taken, and shall continue to take, a deep interest in the success of this work for mental health in Texas, which is more and more recognized as essential to human happiness and welfare." She wanted the family money to help people directly. Direct services, especially for the young, were among her principal goals.

Her outspokenness was tempered by charm and modesty. To Robert L. Sutherland she wrote in 1941, "It is always of interest and concern to me to hear your plans, and when I can be of any little assistance, I am very glad." Ten years later, writing him in regard to plans for a building in honor of her brother Will, she explained that "I was not un-mindful of the appropriateness of such a memorial to him, but I know he would prefer any investment this would entail to be directed toward mental health work which would more closely affect the lives of the people of Texas. At the proper time," she continued, "and I dare hope not too prematurely, a large part of my resources will be put to such use."

When in due time the Will C. Hogg Building was dedicated on The University of Texas campus at Austin, the modest side of Miss Ima took over. She wrote out her remarks of pride and pleasure, but she did not attend the dedication. And on another occasion, "Please don't plan anything for me personally—you know how inadequate I always feel."

Yet Ima Hogg knew her own mind and was not shy about expressing it. When the Mental Health Code was before the legislature in 1957, she wrote a senator friend, "Although I have confidence in Dr. Sutherland and those who have worked on the Mental Health Code, I much prefer coming to my own conclusions, though they may not be as well fortified."

In another letter to Dr. Sutherland, this in 1958, she reviewed the years:

Over the years since the Foundation was established, you and I have carried on a very lively correspondence, in which I never hesitated to express myself because you made me feel free to do so. I have been deeply gratified by the manner in which the work has been conducted. It has been equally gratifying to see the growth of the Foundation's financial status. In the beginning, with very little available resources and a very small staff,

29

Miss Ima, 1959. *Courtesy Conway Studio*

the Foundation carried on a widespread educational program in Mental Health, acquainting the public, for the first time in most cases, with many problems confronting society, as well as giving valuable assistance to organizations related to Mental Health. At present, the Foundation is carrying on such an extended program it would be farfetched for me to attempt any evaluation or analysis of its projected activities. I think all concerned have reason to be proud of the progress and development which has taken place.

Among the work to which she referred were programs for educating and training mental health professionals, for expanding mental health education through a variety of pamphlets and books written in a manner and style that would be understood by anyone who might read them, for expanding state and community services, and for increasing research support. Additional money was obtained in the 1950's from the National Institute of Mental Health and other federal agencies. In the next decade the emphasis was on campus mental health and bettering the lives of the disadvantaged—ethnic minorities, the aged, the very young. Demonstration projects gained increasing support, moving the Foundation toward the more personal direction so favored by Miss Ima.

The emphasis of the Hogg Foundation has shifted through the years to meet current needs. As Dr. Wayne H. Holtzman, the current president, explains, "The fundamental goal of serving all the people of the state within the context of The University of Texas remains. Initial support for innovative ideas is combined with responsibility for well-proven programs. Response is prompt, personal, and considerate to every proposal or cry for help. Given these fundamental premises, there is every reason to have confidence in the Foundation's future, as in its past."

Wayne Holtzman and his wife, Joan, as Robert and Marjorie Sutherland before them, maintained an intimate personal and professional relationship with Miss Hogg throughout the years.

With conductor Arthur Fiedler before a symphony concert, 1966. *Courtesy Houston Post*

IV

Someone once said of Ima Hogg, when she was in her seventies, that "She entered the golden age when all the ships she launched came home bearing gifts." And in a sense this was true. For decades she played a special role in the state, due partly to her unselfish and good ideas, partly to her generosity in music, mental health, and the arts, and partly to her long and active life. She became "the Lady"—listened to, respected, revered. She was, as one a generation her junior expressed it, "a lovely lady . . . with that quality that made it seem that time did not dictate her life—that friendship, leisurely enjoyment of every moment and every interest took precedence over organized activity." And as the wife of a former governor once said, "The governor's wife is usually called the first lady of Texas, but Miss Ima always has been and always will be the first lady of Texas."

She also became the recipient of many awards for her contributions to the people of the state. The National Society of Interior Designers presented her with the Thomas Jefferson Award in recognition of her outstanding contributions to the preservation of American cultural heritage. The National Conference of Christians and Jews honored her with the Brotherhood Award. The Texas Heritage Foundation named her Woman of the Year; the American Association of State and Local History presented her with an Award of Merit for her accomplishments in the preservation and restoration of homes and buildings representative of historic Texas; the National Trust for Historic Preservation cited and honored her. She was appointed a charter member of the Texas State Historical Survey Commission and was one of only two women ever to be named as president of the select Philosophical Society of Texas. And she was well recognized by The University of Texas: named a Distinguished Alumnus in 1962, and recipient of the first Santa Rita Award in 1968.

Perhaps the University of Pennsylvania best expressed the feelings of all who knew her when honoring her:

For her wise recognition that sustained effort is necessary to bring ideals into being . . . For her conviction that a land without history is a land without memories . . . For her impeccable taste and unerring instinct for choosing the best . . . For her steadfast devotion to those special endeavors that enhance the lives of others.

At first she accepted these honors "with trepidation and apprehension." Later she began to enjoy them, often with a twinkle of delight and amusement. Yet always she credited others. As she explained to the audience when accepting an honorary degree from Southwestern University, "In honoring me you honor many other people, for my fulfillment is due to the work of others."

But Ima Hogg was never one to bask in the glory of past accomplishments. Her concern was for the

Miss Ima and Houston Museum of Fine Arts Emeritus Director James Chillman at a dinner party at Bayou Bend, 1970. *Courtesy Houston Chronicle*

33

present, and for the future. Her strength was in ideas, in the long-range vision that saw where she hoped things would lead, and in the tenacity and determination and ability to help lead them there. Never an idle dreamer, she had great skill in getting things started, in organizing and planning how best to achieve her goals. And her goal was to create things of permanent value for the people of Texas.

So, while her "ships came home bearing gifts," she continued to launch new ships, to begin new projects. "There is always something interesting happening these days," she noted, "and deadlines seem to increase." She considered her wealth not as a personal thing but as a trust in her keeping to be used for the good of the people, and she never ran out of ideas for its use. Texas heritage as expressed in furniture and the decorative arts continued to be one of her prime interests.

Bayou Bend, her beloved home which she had long planned as a gift to the city of Houston, was dedicated as a museum in 1966. Miss Ima expressed her hopes and concerns at the dedication: "Texas, an empire in itself, geographically and historically sometimes seems to be regarded as remote or alien to the rest of our nation. I hope in a modest way Bayou Bend may serve as a bridge to bring us closer to the heart of an American heritage which unites us." Speaking of the collection itself, she continued, "May it lead the visitor to delve more deeply into the roots of our American Heritage; and may the visitor be inspired to have a great respect for the cul-

tural life of our early American forefathers. They themselves treasured the beauty and integrity of the objects created by skilled craftsmen according to the artistic and utilitarian standards of the particular era in which they lived."

A speaker at the dedication ceremonies pointed out that "All the beauty we see around us—both inside and outside the building—is essentially the creation of one dedicated person." In addition to the home and furnishings, he was acknowledging the 14 acres on which it stands along a bend of Buffalo Bayou, acreage maintained in formal gardens that are a highlight of Houston's annual Azalea Trail. These gardens are one of the most spectacular examples of Miss Ima's interest in nature and flowers. She had been a charter member of the River Oaks Garden Club, in large part responsible for the club's founding and growth. She had been responsible for seeing that the City of Houston maintained her brother Will's gift of Memorial Park as open parkland. And she delighted in the fact that her gardens provided pleasure for so many. At first she observed the enthusiasm of Azalea Trail visitors from a distance. Later, she took pleasure in sitting on the porch or mingling with the guests. Always a hostess, she saw to it that there was water available for all the visitors and plenty of candy for the children.

In 1957 she presented the Varner-Hogg Plantation, which had been the home her father had loved best, to Texas as a State park. Fully restored, the house looks much as it did when the Hogg family lived there

Bayou Bend. *Courtesy F. Wilbur Seiders*

Drawing room at Bayou Bend. *Courtesy Bayou Bend Collection*

36

at the turn of the century. Furnished with many family antiques and containing some of the Governor's personal documents, it is dedicated to her father's memory and "to those valiant pioneers of each successive period whom he held in such high esteem."

She restored and furnished the first home in which her parents had lived—or perhaps it was an exact replica, for she expressed concern over the authenticity of the dwelling. This "Honeymoon Cottage" in Quitman, now located in the Jim Hogg State Park, she presented to the State of Texas in 1962. She loved the little home in Quitman and enjoyed visiting it from time to time. Whenever she appeared the young children in the neighborhood would shout greetings to "Mizima," and she looked forward to that, too. And she continued to feel a proprietary interest in the Varner-Hogg home in West Columbia. "Check the windows, a hurricane's coming," she once phoned in haste to the director there, long after she had given the home to the State. After she had become widely known for her collections and restorations, she mused, "I began collecting from an aesthetic point of view and out of curiosity. I've made mistakes. But it's all been so much fun. I think I have learned more through furniture and art than anything else."

At the dedication of Bayou Bend Miss Ima had said, "Now I am free to pursue my other projects . . . and to watch the sunsets from a high-rise apartment." It was a new idea, a new project that captured her time and attention when, in 1963, she purchased the Old Stagecoach Inn at Winedale. The building combined German and American elements that predated what was to become a peculiarly Texas culture. Built in 1834, it had been lived in throughout the years but nonetheless had fallen into disrepair. Her first thoughts were to move the Inn to Bayou Bend. Then, partly because of the charm and appropriateness of the community in which it was located and partly because of its setting almost midway between Houston and Austin, she decided to restore it on site. To make sure the restoration met her perfectionist standards, she took a cottage nearby where she could stay on the weekends and supervise the work. And supervise she did—consulting frequently with architect Wayne Bell—climbing over and around construction materials in the Inn and other buildings during every stage of the restoration. Nothing escaped her attention. A carpenter, noticing a sag in the roof, took it upon himself to put up supports to straighten the roofline. When Miss Ima came that weekend, one of her first questions was to ask where the sag was—and her immediate request was to remove the supports so that the roof would remain exactly as it had been built. She was tenacious and strong-willed; as the director of Winedale said, she "exerted a tremendous amount of moral authority."

Ima Hogg was a perfectionist for herself and for others. In each of her many undertakings she read and asked questions, she learned and grew. No task was done halfway. Whether it was a table setting for a

Inspecting the Winedale restoration project, 1967.
Courtesy Houston Chronicle

party or floor boards for a restored house, a fund-raising drive or a gift for a friend, she learned the best way to do it and then followed through. She became an expert in every area in which she was interested, and her interests were many. Miss Ima never stopped learning. To assure the authenticity of the Winedale restoration, she went to New York to study how it could be done, then returned to supervise. When the buildings were completed, she bought and then personally arranged the furniture that was placed in them. She was interested in more than pretty objects; she was intrigued by the process or tools that went into making them, the wood or other material of which they were made. She wanted to know how a piece was used, and why. A true collector, she had the ability to look at a piece of furniture and know if it was a good one, or if there should be something better. Despite poor eyesight in her later years she had unerring taste, with an incredible eye for colors, for design, for the height to hang pictures. Always knowledgeable, sometimes stubborn, she usually made one change in each of the plans for the Winedale property to make her mark on it. "Yet," says the curator, "she was arguable. If you did your homework and could show her the evidence for doing something in a way that differed from hers, she would change her mind. She was the best patron ever to work with."

No trouble or expense was spared in the Winedale restoration. Square nails were ordered from Massachusetts; timber was cut on the Winedale farm to

Sam Lewis house (Stagecoach Inn) at Winedale. *Courtesy Frank Armstrong*

With the polka band at Winedale dedication, 1967.
Courtesy Houston Post

40

assure its similarity to the original. From a small but well preserved piece of wallpaper as a sample, a new roll of wallpaper was produced on special rollers and at great cost so that the living room of one of the homes would be authentic.

The restoration was done for the people of Texas, but Ima Hogg gloried in every step along the way. She enjoyed the German culture and lifestyle in the surrounding countryside. She liked the music, she liked the beer, and she was interested in how the culture manifested itself in Texas—the fraternal and singing societies, the language, the foods. From this interest grew the plan to make Winedale a center for the study of ethnic cultures which migrated to Texas in the early 19th century—the German, Czech, Polish, Swiss, and Scandinavian people who were the settlers of Central Texas. In 1965 she presented the Winedale property, with an endowment for its support and with a concept of ethnic heritage for its direction, to The University of Texas as the Museum of Cultural History. At the dedication, an event attended by dignitaries from both the state and the nation, guests were seated under a large canopy and entertained by a German oompah band. Then, following an introduction of the prestigious visitors, Miss Ima made a few remarks. She spoke primarily about the methods used in restoring the Inn and the ways in which she hoped it would be used. After expressing appreciation to the many people who took part in the restoration, she concluded by paying tribute to the artisans, "without whom this project

Parlor of restored house at Winedale. *Courtesy Jim Bones*

41

would not have been possible." At her request the proud carpenters rose to accept her thanks.

Music, through her love for it, became an integral part of the Winedale program. The museum sponsored the first two music festivals led by pianist James Dick, who was one of her protégés; and it began an annual spring music festival which continues to be one of its major events. Miss Ima herself enjoyed playing on the Steinway there, performing a few Bach selections at the Christmas party each year. And when, in the late 1960s, she helped restore the old German wooden organ in the little church in the nearby community of Round Top, she climbed up to the small square steeple to play the organ for the townspeople assembled below.

She also introduced her love of nature, of flowers and gardens, to the Winedale acres. All of the plantings are authentic replicas of the period they represent. From an 1861 almanac she learned about historic landscape gardening, then personally laid out a star-shaped flowerbed in the front yard of one of the historic houses on the site. Miss Ima continued to be interested in Winedale, visiting it every few weeks until just before her final trip abroad. One time when she had invited a guest to join her, they lunched at the small cafe in Round Top. As they got out of the car to enter the restaurant, the chauffeur took out a large picnic basket. Always the gracious hostess, Miss Ima had brought along some fishhouse punch to make the occasion festive.

As Ima Hogg pursued her dreams, as she set the example that inspired and cajoled others into carrying out her plans, she was always more than the imposing though somewhat shy public figure so widely known. For she was a very human lady, one with compassion and wit and a manner that charmed all who spent any time in her presence. "She was so concerned about my staff," said the curator of the Texas archives. "She was conscious of the fact that it wasn't too difficult to impose her will on others, so she tried to put people at ease. She was great with the young staff members." "She'd know how you felt just by looking at you," noted Lucius Broadnax, her chauffeur and general helper for 30 years. "She always tried to ease the strain, was always kind and considerate." And Mr. Broadnax also well remembers how, on their many antiquing trips, she taught him how to recognize good furniture, how to feel the grain of the wood, how to care for it with a special polish they made themselves.

Though she appreciated attentions, Miss Ima was more concerned about others than about herself. "She was one of the most meticulous persons about writing notes of appreciation," commented a long-time associate and friend. "She acknowledged kindnesses immediately, and always in longhand." Once, after an illness, when she had received attentions too numerous to acknowledge individually, she ordered cards printed to thank her many friends. However, ordinary cards wouldn't do. She insisted they be printed in red, to be attractive and cheerful was more important than protocol.

She had a gift for harmony. Those who worked with her stayed not just for years but for decades. In meetings she had a knack for keeping others agreeable even though opinions differed. "To work with Miss Ima was to grow yourself," said one friend. "She brought out virtues in people, helped them acquire patience and tolerance through her example. She was an inspiration—and a challenge."

And she was fun. When close to age 90, she attended a circus and had a wonderful time. Afterward she wanted to meet the lion tamer, the tightrope walker, the man who trained the horses to keep time to music. She wanted to know how they accomplished these feats, how they worked with the animals. She enjoyed many things; she also enjoyed finding out how they worked.

The one thing about which she had no humor was her name. She was upset by references to a sister named Ura, which began as what she considered a cruel political joke when her father ran for governor while she was still a small child. Jane Zivley, her secretary and friend for more than 25 years, well remembers how Miss Ima was plagued throughout her life by letters, phone calls, and comments about her name and the names of imaginary sisters. However, she rarely spoke of it. When introducing herself to people she would always pause slightly, "My name is Ima . . . Hogg." Apparently her father never considered the effect of the combination of his daughter's given and family names. He wanted to honor his brother and took the name from lines of a poem the brother had written: "A Southern girl, whose winsome grace and kindly, gentle mien, betrayed a heart more beauteous than her face. Ah! she was fair; the Southern skies were typed in Ima's heavenly eyes."

Only when she was well along in years and considering the possibility of writing her memoirs did Miss Ima record the story of her naming:

My uncle Thomas Elisha had died not long before and to honor his memory I was named for the heroine of his epic poem about the Civil War, "The Fate of Marvin." Grandfather Stinson lived 15 miles from Mineola and news travelled slowly. When he learned of his granddaughter's name he came trotting to town as fast as he could to protest but it was too late. The christening had taken place, and Ima I was to remain.

For all who knew Miss Ima, the humor of her name was soon overlooked. The saying in Houston was that newcomers realized they were becoming real Houstonians when Miss Ima's name no longer seemed odd.

Ima Hogg's love and knowledge of music continued unabated throughout the years. One of her favorite forms of entertainment was to have a dinner party before the Monday night symphonies, which she attended regularly. The guests who came for the early dinner usually included prominent townspeople and special visitors. Afterwards, they would adjourn to the symphony, where they were seated in her box for six. In later years, when the symphony moved to the new Jones Hall, they sat in the orchestra seats, which she considered acoustically better.

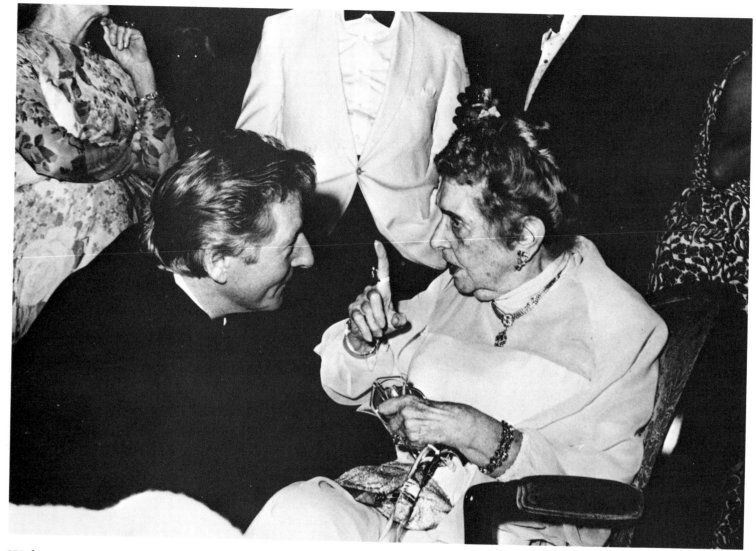

With Houston Symphony guest conductor Danny Kaye,
1974. *Courtesy Houston Chronicle*

Even when she was losing her hearing, her critical ear remained sharp. A guest at one of these occasions will never forget when, after hearing the first few bars of Beethoven's Seventh Symphony, Miss Ima said, in a stage whisper audible for 30 rows, "That's much too fast." "And what's more, she was right," he added with a chuckle.

Entertaining was one of her many skills. "Dinners were her favorite," recalls Broadnax, who helped at almost all of the occasions, "but there were all those cocktail parties, teas, coffees. As a hostess she was one of the finest. She wanted her guests to enjoy themselves, and she saw to it that they always did."

While most of her entertaining served a purpose —to bring together people who were interested in mental health or music or fine arts or museums or gardening or some other one of her many philanthropic interests—there was an informal side to Miss Ima that a few friends were privileged to know. "We liked to have Sunday dinner together," recalls a friend of many years. "She'd come to our house and we'd listen to the symphony." She smiled as she continued, "We'd all three take naps at the beginning, then we'd wake up, enjoy the rest of the music and discuss it over supper. We kept this up until three or four years ago."

The lady mused a bit. "One lovely thing she did through the years was on Christmas Eve, when she invited her close friends and their families over. We sang carols, played games, and had supper. The same group of friends attended over the years, and as the children grew up they'd bring their dates to the party. Ima would play the piano; she had a lovely touch."

To those who met Miss Ima in her later years, she was not only a lady, but a regal one. "I don't suppose I'll ever again come as close to being entertained by royalty," one man exclaimed. "She was a Southern lady with Western toughness." Regal looking, always stylish, she had a special quality that made her stand out wherever she was. "I knew her in an official context, in what might be called pompous situations," commented a University official, "but she was not at all a pompous person." Formal in addressing others, concerned about doing things properly, Ima Hogg was nonetheless a liberal in the sense that she was concerned about all the people of Texas. For though from her many travels abroad she was truly a citizen of the world, she was, as someone said, "a worldly Texan." Her attention remained focused on Texas; she developed her interests and channeled them into efforts that would benefit the lives of her fellow citizens.

V

The Houston Symphony honored Miss Ima on her 90th birthday with a special concert, highlighted by the performance of an old friend of hers, Artur Rubinstein. Not only did she admire Rubinstein's piano artistry, but she also agreed with his philosophy of life.

I am passionately involved in life. I love its change, its color, its movement. To be alive, to be able to see, to walk, to have houses, music, paintings—it's all a miracle. I have adopted the technique of living from miracle to miracle. What people get out of me is an outlook on life which comes out in my music.

In her Christmas cards that year Ima Hogg printed Rubinstein's philosophy, followed by a note of her own: "A Way of Life—May you find the same zest for life which Artur Rubinstein so beautifully exemplifies."

No one better exemplified a joyous and productive approach to living, a more positive outlook on life, than Ima Hogg. Her interests, her unfailing concern for others, her ideas for the future never diminished. She became known for her phone calls, getting in touch with friends every few weeks to discuss problems affecting youth or schools, to ask a question, pursue a thought, and almost always to present an idea. "She once called to ask if the wildflowers were in bloom at Winedale," the curator recalled.

"I was busy and it seemed unimportant so I glanced out the window and replied 'yes, ma'am.' But she apparently caught the tone in my voice and wasn't about to be put off that way. 'How many?' she immediately demanded." It was difficult to put anything over on Miss Ima.

Still busy with her many interests, though beginning to fail in hearing and sight, Ima Hogg left for England shortly after her 93rd birthday to attend some concerts and visit museums. It was a happy trip until it was marred by an accident, a fall as she was stepping into a taxi one evening on the way to the theater. Taken to the hospital with a broken hip, she hastened to reassure the cab driver and the friends who gathered around her. "Whatever happens," she told them, "remember that it is the way it was meant to be. I'm doing what I want to do. I'm where I want to be. I have no regrets."

She never returned from that trip. After her death, letters came from throughout the country, from Mexico, from England. Articles appeared praising her many gifts, her "long list of achievements from civic to music, which have substantially changed our lives for the better. But," that author continued, "her greatest gift didn't cost a cent—it was her outlook on life. She worried, but she hoped as well. 'I have no answers,' she once wrote, 'only a burning desire to see something encouraging happen.'" Miss Ima had become a legend in her own lifetime; she had lived long and well, and she would be missed.

Some years ago, in accepting an award from The University of Texas, Miss Ima remarked that "members of our family grew up in Austin under the shadow of The University of Texas campus. By precept and experience within its walls, we learned to cherish its ideals. I realize, in choosing me to honor, it was not so much for my personal worth as for the fact that I represent members of my family whom you wish to remember, and through them, you have identified me with certain forces and ideas which I am gratified you hold worthy."

That was Miss Ima's modest view, but others felt differently. "Among those Texans," former University of Texas Chancellor Harry Ransom once said, "who have brought the light of the mind, heart's courage, and complete dedication of strong will to the welfare of all kinds of people, Miss Hogg is not, if you are willing to believe Miss Hogg, very special. Perhaps not, except for the patent fact that in Texas history there has been no other Texan quite like her." It seems unlikely that there ever will be.

Miss Ima's 90th birthday party, Winedale, 1970. *Courtesy Houston Chronicle*

Type set by G & S TYPESETTERS
Printed by CAPITAL PRINTING COMPANY
Paper supplied by LONE STAR PAPER COMPANY
Bound by CUSTOM BOOKBINDERS
Design by WILLIAM D. WITTLIFF, *The Encino Press*